Rhapsody for Lessons Learned or Remembered

Rhapsody for Lessons Learned or Remembered

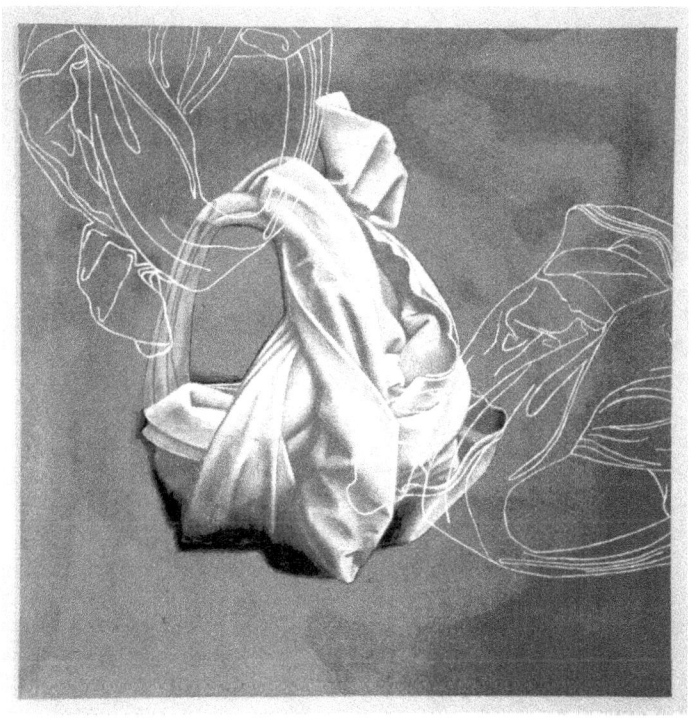

Georgia Ann Banks-Martin

Plain View Press
P. O. 42255
Austin, TX 78704

plainviewpress.net
sb@plainviewpress.net
512-441-2452

Copyright Georgia Banks-Martin, 2010. All rights reserved under International and Pan-American Copyright Conventions. No part of this book may be reproduced or distributed in any form or by any means, or stored in a data base or retrieval system, without written permission from the author. All rights, including electronic, are reserved by the author and publisher.

ISBN: 978-1-935514-64-0
Library of Congress Number: 2010934935

Cover art: "Ghost Cacoon," by Samantha Ainsley, www.samainsley.com

Cover design by Susan Bright

Contents

Evening Guitar	15
Railroad Station	16
Remembering an Autumn Day	17
Apple-Picking	18
Zinnias	19
Tradition	20
La Volière	21
Dreams 2	22
Madonna and Child	23
Dancing Doll	24
Mother's Lessons	25
The Floor-Scrapers	26
Wishing for a Fairy	27
Patience	28
Ava	29
Montgomery Stairs	31
Portrait of American Hope	32
Conjure Woman	33
Birds of the Bagaduce	34
Seasonal Rain	35
South Carolina Morning or Cape Cod Evening	36
Denial of Appeal	37

Woman in Green Coat	38
Still Life	39
Breach of Contract	41
On the Terrace	42
Self-Examination	43
Cotton Candy	44
Early Morning	45
Seasonal Longings	46
Terrace of a Café	47
Woman with a Pearl Necklace	48
Cornflowers and Ears of Corn	49
Madame X	50
Ballet Dancer	51
End of Season	52
Earth Warming Mexico	53
Make Your Move	54
Two Note Song	55
The Birth of Venus	56

After Seeing Agostina Segatori in the Café du Tambourin   57
Heart Trouble   58
Death Dancing   59
Portrait of Père Tanguy   61
Tired   62
On Highway 80   63
Grand Central Station   64
Piano Lesson   65
The Persistence of Time   66

Notes   67
About the Author   75

Acknowledgements

I would like to thank the editors of the following publications in which these poems first appeared, sometimes in earlier versions, sometimes with other titles. As well as the poets who have taken time to read, offer feedback, and suggest places to submit often without knowing that the poems were a part of this project.

"Evening Guitar," "Zinnias," *African-American Review;* "Montgomery Stairs," *After Shocks: The Poetry of Recovery for Life-Shattering Events*; "On an Autumn Day," "Seasonal Longings," "Seasonal Rain," *Fieralingue*; "Portrait of American Hope," "Woman in Green Coat," *Möbius: The Poetry Journal*; "Dancing Doll," "The Floor-Scrapers," "Terrance of a Café on Montmartre," *Munyori Literary Journal*; "Tired," *Pearl Magazine*; "South Carolina Morning," *Prick of the Spindle;* "Conjure Woman," "Birds of the Bagaduce," "Apple-Picking," "Breach of Contract," *Thanal Online*; "Piano Lesson," *The 2009 Limestone Dust Poetry Festival Anthology;* "The Birth of Venus," *Up the Staircase;* "Madonna and Child," *Xavier Review.*

Thank you to Amanda Surkont, Athena Kildegaard, Audrey Friedman, Carol Dorf, Farideh Hassanzadeh-Mostafavi, Janet McCann, Katherine Drubek, Lisa Heeg, Louisa Hen, Nancy Connolly, Peggy Miller, Lori A. May, Julene T. Weaver, Alan Michael Parker, Brighde Mullins, and Peter Stitt.

Dedicated to my mom

Inez L. Banks

1930-2009

*To equate identity with race and culture
is to deny the power of the imagination
which can be the empathic bridge
between nations, culture, and individuals.*

      Julius Lester

Evening Guitar

Someone loaned me a book
filled with images of Mississippi,
of people washing clothes,
fishing, pressing hair.

A collage stretches across
its cover: a divided blue room,
one side filled with daily living:
bucket, broom, chicken, lamp,
a guitar for Saturday's singing.

Behind the partition, a woman sits
rubbing the top of her foot
while reaching for a blue dress
piled on the seat of a straight back
undersized chair.

The book smells of smoke,
from the coal burning stove,
sharing the table with the lady's
porcelain tea service,
the pages repeatedly read,
savored between long sips.

Railroad Station

Those leaving the towns where father and mother
labored in fields without being offered a yard of thread spun
from the cotton they pulled, have assembled.
Packed: Hopes of work, three bedroom homes,
water heated in water tanks, classrooms.
In the far corner a wife whispers to her husband,
What if here is better than there?
A girl pulled along by her mother like a stubborn puppy,
There are nice people where we are going. You will make new friends.
Brother holds his stomach hoping Mama
brought some cornbread and greens.
A man sits atop his luggage like a bird hatching an egg.
Father stands silently holding cases in each hand like dumbbells.

Remembering an Autumn Day

Two stray cats are making love
beneath my bedroom window.
The dogwood blooms have floated
down to the streets from heavy laden boughs;
the sun shines just warm enough to remind me
of air-conditioning, long cotton dresses,
twine edged sandals.
Soon star-like buds will appear
on the fence born of a vine that during
the first week of fall had continued climbing
hoping the sun wouldn't turn its back,
the wind would only stroke still green leaves,
allowing them a few more hours,
before rain, twisting, tearing,
tumbling though unpaved alleys—
the shedding of seeds.

Apple-Picking

Each year Mama chooses a day
to pick apples, the day
when she doesn't have to tug
to free one from its place.

That's the day she climbs the tree
and shakes its branches
while I weave between bean poles,
turnips, and collards,
collecting the fallen fruit,

she doesn't mind if it's bruised
so she shakes hard
but some always remain
attached to their boughs.

My cousin uses a long handled
picker to pluck those so when
my friends come over to play
the last apples won't get trampled.

We place the fruit into bushel baskets.
When mine is full I choose a small apple
to eat. Inside it is white, and warm,
the juice sweet and sticky.

I only eat one knowing that tonight,
Mama will open the last jar
of jelly from last year,
the jelly she saved for us to spread
on slices of toast today
after we have picked the apples.

Zinnias

I remember their scent,
their peach fuzz stems—
I remember summer mornings
picking them along Cane River.
A bouquet of flattened petals,
purple, blue and gold on reclaimed,
tea-washed linen.
I remember Mother
placing them between Bible pages
as if she were hiding presents
too precious for Sears Roebuck.

Tradition

I placed a fresh rose on Grandma's grave,
not knowing on Mother's Day she wore a silk bud.
A simple stem long separated from the plastic
frilly foliage, first worn with a three-button jacket,
skirt barely pooling around her feet,
on her wedding day. There was no money
for freshly wired roses and it didn't concern her:
cut blossoms never live to bloom another year.

La Volière

In the store window stands a manikin
with sawed off head leaving a prefect neck
on an armless torso that precisely mimics
the curve of a woman's waist;
the breast a hill on a flat plain
a rest for grabbing fingers welded
to a full skirt of rebar; purity unburned paper,
stored inside the firebox of a smothering home.

Dreams 2

No one wanted wedding cake without a wedding,
without watching a bride leave the church,
float down the stairs to her new husband
waiting with arms open as if he expects
her to land in them,
to have, to hold
vow broken before it could be uttered.

Without a daughter to inherit my loathing
I sit in the shadows of this room
my new suitor's kisses resisted;
invitations slip from my hand.
One day the postman will stop delivering them.

Madonna and Child

My priest said Jesus had golden hair,
was the son of Mary and Joseph;
was crucified for my sins—and I believed,

not knowing children attending segregated
schools learned white people were good;
black bad, that black children preferred
pink dolls to those who were chestnut,

but I knew my olive skin
(not even when the summer sun
glazed it caramel) never hid my blue veins;

I had run my finger along Mother's arm,
looking for the same slender cables,
disappointed the mahogany didn't break,
had asked, which five-and-dime
she bought me from,
wondering if it were Cunningham's
where she got my blonde baby doll
whose hair I pen-curled 'til I was twelve,

'til mother bought me a doll
with light brown skin, a pink swimsuit;
tan lines, long sandy hair I could braid,

but Jesus still was a yellow-haired baby boy,
held by a veiled woman in blue robes,
seated on a throne,
never the son of a mother who knelt over
a crib, wearing a bonnet, full black skirt,
white servant's apron,
living in a one room house.

Dancing Doll

Some say Sambo wears
                bright reds
      blues and greens
           dances
on street corners for large groups of people

      grinning
as he did when snitching to the master
encouraging him to beat his slaves
in return for a fairer share of tea
      potatoes
           meats

      grinning
when writing hateful notes
taping them to his dorm room door
      later saying
"I found these after class today"

Forums were held
      programs created
           deans declared
     dangerous racists

but I remember meeting Sambo
on his way to eat pancakes topped with butter
made from the flesh of three trickster tigers
a boy who had no right
to wear *a red coat*
      blue trousers
   shoes with crimson soles and *linings*
      to carry a green umbrella

Mother's Lessons

    Oatmeal
          raisins
                  toast
Bible reading by Daddy
before we wave from the window
'til his lean body blends into the tree line
before he begins cutting the grass
watering the roses that welcome
students to the university we will attend
while mother polishes the silver tea service
we don't use
helps sis practice reading skills
me to draw lines of As
the one letter word that always wants something
A yard
          A swing set with seesaw
A couple of children   seesawing
        seesawing
the day away

The Floor-Scrapers

The stripping has begun,
Long smooth strokes, use long smooth strokes,
says the older man to his apprentice,
as if all should be respected:

the spots of indigo paint long covered
with a rose pink rug,

the places my tap shoes pocked
the floor's face like acne,
each time I jiggled my feet for family friends
whose lips knew the expected words so well
it was a burden to stay silent,
She's a star—
Delightful, just delightful—

the day mother bought my first heels
made me walk with a dictionary on my head
till the book kept its place,
Shoulders back,
      chin up,
step light,
      no one should hear you coming.

Wishing for a Fairy

The Tooth Fairy never came to my house
Mother didn't believe in her
Mother plucked my teeth from their sockets
after I tried to yank them out with sewing thread

I would keep the tooth in an amber bottle
hoping that before the week's end
Mother would allow me
to place it beneath my pillow
and wait for my fairy

The one with large eyes the one I had made extra pretty
by outlining every detail of her ball gown
with a black crayon
the spots on her wings
        sea green
                and burnt orange

wait for her to sneak into my room
slip her slender hand beneath my pillow
place a few
                quarters
       dimes
                nickels
to be spent on a cone of swirly ice-cream
a pack of bubble gum

Patience

Before Mother became ill
I remember her spending
days pulling needles
loaded with heavy cotton thread
through bits of fabric fashioning
flowers from tattered ties
shirts and trousers
getting up to pour milk
shell pecans
beat a few eggs
mix butter and flour together

Before her hands began to tremble
She drew flowers on pages of the newspaper
some were smaller than her thumb
bending toward earth the weight of their number
too much for the twig from which they sprung
each shape had to be perfect
before she laid them on the squares
she had cut from a worn-out tablecloth
each tear drop petal covered
with a sheet of lapis blue paper
traced with a small wheel
cut out like shapes from one of my first grade color sheets

Now unfinished quilts are stretched
over and between wooden frames
white silver striped china visible
through the cabinet's glass door
wait for the day
the shuffling feet
the clumsy shoulders
the trembling hands
can again be disciplined

Ava

Willis is looking for a woman
a young woman to marry
says he can't find one who knows
what his mother knew
        eight-o-clocks
                not touch- me-nots
        elephant ears
                not calla lilies
     impatiens
            not pansies

He wants a wife whose cotton shirt
        is hidden by a kitchen apron
                large patch pocket at the hem
wears a broad brim
        sun bleached hat
           blanket ribbon tied in bow

                double bead earrings purchased
                     from the same general store as his
                        screwdriver lawnmower
        saw
greeting him wide-eyed
        in the evening
with fresh flowers
     from her garden
        pink
            purple
      petals
spilling over the brim of her wooden bucket

She will place them in the chandelier
that hung above his mother's wedding table
reminding him to always
                              protect the roots
                                pack the soil
                              water the garden

Montgomery Stairs

The morning sun lends
a gentle glow to this historic
street whose blue markers
offer far few words to excise
the ghosts of men marching,
wearing perfectly pointed
white hats, veils draping
their faces and necks, armed
with rocks and hand-made
bombs, they take the homes
of Negroes leaving behind
these sagging stairs
upon which I will not allow
my dog to piss——
something has to be sacred.

Portrait of American Hope

The dead and living were left floating
like boats that sail the Great Lakes
when Katrina washed New Orleans away
as if she were out of fashion.

Survivors littered fields, faces marred
by frowns and tears, but one woman sat,
head and shoulders draped
with a red, white and blue flag.

Conjure Woman

I read a book of stories
about enchanted grapevines,
forsaken wives and cultured clubs.

Its cover has begun to curl
trying to hide from me
the featured woman's hair
long, black, asymmetrically parted,

Her eyes which watch,
which question why
I have come
are borrowed from her mother's master,

her cheeks well defined
borrowed from an unknown Native American,

her broad shoulders, large hands—
one held half-way up
as if I have interrupted her—borrowed.

Birds of the Bagaduce

I often visit our favorite Hartley,
dream the largest boat is ours,
remember the first trip we took
on my twenty-eighth birthday.

While sweet smoke from your pipe
hovered around our shoulders
like a lacy shawl,

we listened for the water's
gurgling, the humming
of dragon fly wings,
frogs croaking,

white bellied gulls
snatching smelts from the water,
snagging rides aboard Smith Cove-
bound boats.

The gallery owner
wants to make me a print,
ship it to me overnight.

But it's not the painting
I want to remember.

Seasonal Rain

Where the bus stops there's a sign.
A small rectangle shaped piece of metal
hanging from a pole.
There's a house with a wooden fence
around the yard.
It's the type of fence that once
might have been white washed.
One board is missing
forming the kind of gap one might expect
to see a white dog
with a black ring around one eye run
trying to catch up with a gang
of mischievous children.
But today I see a rain swollen pond,
a strand of morning glory twisting
around the tall silver grass
decorating it with small orange stars
while white lilies huddle beneath
low hanging leaves.

South Carolina Morning or Cape Cod Evening

for Timeka

All night I've been awake wishing
I could be one of Hopper's women,
maybe the one waiting outside her front door for a man
who is always late and won't notice how like tracing paper
the fabric of her red dress chases each curve,
or even the one who stiffly stands near her husband
ignored as he plays with his dog,
it is easier then telling the truth about where you've been,
I would rather be waiting, forever, than mourning my husband.

Denial of Appeal

In an almost deserted mall,
a woman passed as I
perched on the edge
of an indoor waterfall.

Brows arched, brushed-
penciled.

Eyes, held open
by a wide band of liquid liner-
long faux lashes,

mouth red as candied cherries.

The man across from me said,
women don't need make-up,
as he placed his hands in his
front pockets,
gave his pants a little tug,
trying to hide his erect penis.

I felt my lips stretch into a smile
while I wondered if a group
of plain-faced, nude women,
splashing in the fountain's pool,
would be less appealing.

Woman in Green Coat

The park was typical today, couples strolling,
holding hands, kissing, one woman watching,
I knew what she was thinking, I used to have
the same thoughts. I should have told her love
comes with fear and anxiety.

I should have told her how I wish for calls
from the bill collector, asking for Mary Gregory,
as if I would say "She's here today, please hold,"
the salesman who used to trick me into buying
seven-year magazine subscriptions,
filled my mail with socialites jailed for DUI.

I long for those calls like some women crave chocolate,
not the ones beginning: *Father has fallen, EMS is on the way,*
He's having breathing problems but won't go to the hospital,
His behavior has become erratic, his options: limited,
The calls that suggest I take comfort in knowing
he's going to a nursing home, not returning to the house
where he pulled hair from his wife's gray head,
where he gave uncle a black eye,
where we took his gun away,
fearing suicide.

Still Life

After three months of tests
        four hours of surgery
one week in the hospital
      my desk has become burdened by *Get Well Wishes*
and care packages

Above the envelopes and boxes hangs a picture
            of an ink-well and feather
                    a first edition leather bound book
     illegible letter——
            perhaps a hint of what another tried to write while
recovering
from an illness

Overwhelmed
      the writer folded the note into quarters
              prepared it for delivery
 retrieved it—opened it——re-read what he had written
              left it— un-mailed
hoping the words would stop failing
      knowing the words that would come later would be better—
but they weren't

The thought saddens me
      I begin to wish pixies were real
            wish hundreds of them would slip from the book
     make a ski-jump by
         propping plume against well
 land on the cards signed
The Sunriser Sunday School class—
We'll be in the chapel praying for you!
Heritage Hair Cutters—
Hope your recovery is short. Next cut on Us!

My room would fill with squeaky giggling as sheets of paper
lift from my stationary box
bending
twisting
hydraulically moving
up down up
as small plumes inscribe each with the message I couldn't
the one that will always mean
more than
Thank You

Breach of Contract

Our contract says all life ends,
though the living don't plan to honor
the agreement.

Antelope outrun cheetahs,
weeds become immune to herbicides,
roaches flee when overhead lights
switch on.

Humans allow machines to breathe for them
'til tired lungs are rested,
holding to the world like
a blooming vine
coiled around its own urn—

On the Terrace

The *baby* was a girl,
sixteen toes, two claws,
a yellow-eyed tabby swaddled
in her new daddy's jersey,
I name Rachel Redshirt,
as I wonder if he dreams
of having a daughter,
brown hair, liquid eyes?

Would he buy two hats for Easter
one that sits high on her head,
the other for me with upturned brim?

Should I decorate them with daisies
from my garden?

Self-Examination

My wife says, *Wear your smock*
in the studio. Wouldn't want paint
on your shirt when you get to the office!
as she pulls the full white cloth over
my head as if she were dressing our daughter's
daisy circle clown.

She kisses the back of my neck.
It seems I do everything she expects—
earn extra money, feed the children, her and me.

Yet the living room is painted mauve,
the kitchen yellow,
bedroom blue,
My studio! A pale green.
Why! I silently yell.

Paintings by other artists hang over our fireplace.
The mantle overflows with nameless objects
in the corner the ironing board stands,
next to a pile of white shirts and little dresses,
then I remember why I never complain.
How can I complain about the way someone else
creates art?

Cotton Candy

I don't know why wafted hair,
packaged in snap close bags,
smells of French vanilla and fresh strawberries,
reminds me of the carnival,
the Ferris wheel from which I can hold hands
with a constellation,
bumper cars glittering like my nail polish,
game booths where a dollar buys four chances
to toss a ping pong ball from five feet
into one of fifty small containers.
I always lose, but never miss the woman pulling spheres
of woolly sugar, bigger than my head,
from her silver spinning bowl;
never leave the park 'til she has my last two dollars;
the single bills I rolled into small rods,
twisted the ends of my hair around them when I had been bored.
Never leave before Leo walks across the sky.

Early Morning

I hardly have my shoes on
before you are jumping,
spinning in tight circles around me.

Out the side-door we race down the drive.
A stop at the corner means a Spider Lily
gets extra water,
me, a chance to catch-up,
roll a bit more of your leash
into the palm of my hand.

Side by side we walk
the block then back.
I sit in my favorite chair,
open my laptop.

You paw my leg,
'till I have scooted over,
forcing my thigh into the side arm
your small body fills the space.

I stroke your back my fingers search
for bits of leaves, pine needles, dirt
clinging to your long silky coat.

You prop your head on my thigh
as if it were a pillow
and close your brown eyes,
our morning ritual has nothing
to do with peeing;
everything to do with time shared.

Seasonal Longings

Friends write to say an unexpected snow
has covered the roads in Detroit and Chicago,
while outside my window, trees
have turned deep green, irises are opening.

I try picturing myself as a child
in France, during late winter, early spring,
Mother watching me from the doorway,
as I use my hula-hoop like a jump-rope,
without caring that I might get dirty,
that she will have to wash, starch, press
the white suit I'm wearing,

but I always long to put on a coat,
like the one I wore as a child,
pale orange with stitched down pleats
across the shoulder blades,
four over-sized buttons in front and a belt,

to run outside look for ice to slide on,
slush to jump up and down in,
maybe even a place to lie down.

Terrace of a Café

The drive from Munich to Merano covers,
with sheets of hazy vellum,
my memories of Cinderella's twenty-seven blue,
gold-leafed towers,
replaces them with castles whose spires reach
into the sky like Cathedrals
I will not forget,

though the walk up, then downhill,
dragging overfilled bags,
the comment I made that Merano,
its window boxes overflowing
with fuzzy leafed geraniums
looked like Montgomery,
the picnic table with white starched cloth,
where I ate in an outdoor room,
will be,

'till on the plane home I begin to write
and remember the eatery
where waiters wear waistcoats, black pants,
stiff ankle-long aprons,
where I ordered shrimp with tomato pesto,
not because I missed home's sweetness,
but because I wanted to know if it tasted the same.

Woman with a Pearl Necklace

Single strands of small beads
hanged low from my aunt's neck
like trim on a Christmas tree
She said I reached for them
as I sat on her lap
my face glowing like a silk lantern
She didn't tell me about
                the ponds
                        added sand
            forced shells
      life given
                life taken
the noose fitted perfectly to my neck

Cornflowers and Ears of Corn

On my way to school
I pass brown fields
many are overgrown with grass
that grew on resting land and died
at the end of the season.

While other lots
look as if someone has placed
long poles in the earth
to display a collection of small
blue enameled pens.

Flowers waiting to be sold
to women who want to dress-up
their simple bell shaped hats.

But the sticks are tall stocks of corn.
Field corn— dead since last year
when little green winged bugs
began to nibble the sweet kernels
as if they were hired reapers
instructed to leave nothing behind.

Madame X

X, letter, not last name,
a substitute for a name
no longer wanted.

Madame, French for Mrs.
drop the *e* and in English
she's a whore.

Sargent dropped the left strap
of shiny gems off her shoulder,
plunged the neck line,
laid bare the full chest,
cinched the already small waist,
had her coyly twist her arm.

When scandal ensued,
he returned the jewels
to their place,
kept the name,
maintained the portrait
was the best he'd ever done.

Ballet Dancer

My jewelry box plays Swan Lake
while the ballerina turns without noticing
the soda stained sheet music beneath her;
hymns to play Sunday at Mt. Zion,
next week New Hope Baptist,
maybe St. James AME the week after.

Mother insists I play for choirs,
music will give me security,
a skill that will always be needed,
I might even open my own studio,
fill it with students, she says.

Some measures are blurred,
but my fingers know the keys
just as my mind knows a dancer
satin ribbon holding loose braids,
fitted top fastened with fabric buttons
like a bride's gown,
tulle skirt, milky pink tights,
back arched, arms locked behind me,
feet in fourth position.

End of Season

Hours before Labor Day's fun
could begin, a hurricane
visited the coast.

Upon arrival he threw sand,
poured water onto floors,
ripped signs from walls,
converted homes to boats.

He played all day most of the night,
fell asleep in early morning,

Charlene's Seafood Stand,
with a little sweeping, a lot of mopping
was ready for diners by noon,
but no one wanted to wade through mud,
climb over shingles, bricks, and glass,
not even on the last holiday of the year.

So Charlene leaned her chairs against their tables,
conceding white dresses, swimsuits, and straw hats,
had been forced into retirement;
she would be happy remembering
the day a stray ball bounced onto table ten,
pushing just-fried shrimp into Mrs. Gee's lap,
hearing her shrill voice declare
Grease on my new swim dress!

Earth Warming Mexico

Red splashed across a stretched canvas,
an invitation to pull out your burlap tunic,
your best jeans, thigh high boots,
the tiger mask you and papa made from wire,
strips of newspaper, homemade flour paste.

Dance to the violin,
mark the rhythms with your whip,
tell how papa sent his dog
to hunt down the big cat that trampled his corn.

After, when morning is an infant,
you can rest in the cool stillness of the pink hills,
where the noise of ongoing parties
becomes your lullaby.

Make Your Move

He brushed his hat like a butler might
before placing it on his shaven head.

The jersey that once hung
like a sack from his shoulders,
oversized jeans, brand-name sneakers,
replaced by a button-down shirt,
pleated pants, mid-priced loafers.

It's a two-hour drive to town
where he grew up stuffing sandwich bags
with black and red discs into his pockets,
carrying an 8x8 grid folded in half
to the biggest tree in the park,

playing checkers with his dad
he would abandon first
for frat houses, dreaded hair,
pre-professional tests;
        then bids,
licenses,
        contracts,
twenty minutes to dart 'cross town,
twenty minutes before the older man
will pull a red stool to the table
move one black piece forward.

Two Note Song

I
Daddy called me a harlot for wearing red lipstick
and purple eyeliner to church one Sunday.

Later that week my dance teacher yelled! *You walk like cows.*
She stopped our class in the hall; made us stand in line
while she walked up and down, thighs silently bouncing from side to side,
heels clicking instead of stomping.

When Daddy saw what I had learned I was grounded for a week.

II
I saw a painting of three nude women.
One perched on a marble top seat
that curved around a fountain,
drying her foot while the other women watched.

I turn the corner and find Mrs. Sitwell leaning
against her living room table in a beaded gown.
I wonder how long she spent in the debtor's prison.

I wonder how a woman gets the confidence
to be seen without clothes and shoes,
without pearls and diamonds.

III
How I can stop myself from dreaming of being surrounded
by a mob of men who cover me with yellow sticky notes
that bear the words slut, and whore.

The Birth of Venus

When does sex become dirty?
After the orgy when you see pictures of your mother
holding you in your white lace gown
at the altar rail, bishop dabbing your forehead,
declaring you a child of Christ baptized,
buried, risen with him.
Does it happen when you notice a woman,
admit you want to lick her labia,
cup her upright tits, suck her nipples,
knowing you are a woman too?

After Seeing Agostina Segatori in the Café du Tambourin

I dropped my robe
checked my thighs,
the stretch marks are still there,
so are those twin freckle-size moles,
dark brown ink spots on my deep tan skin.

I skip my navel, I know the ring is crooked
four years of eating pizza, chips, cheese cake
will do that.

I think. If I go to one more spinning class
pump a little more iron, each week,
by Christmas I will be skinny

a little closer to forty
a little closer
never to being the girl
wearing her dark hair beneath a head rag,
alone at a too-small café table,
cigarette half-smoked
half-smothered away.

Heart Trouble

A man outside my office
sings of summer time.
His heart so weak his skin
has turned grayish blue,

Good old summer time,
When your day's work is over
Then you are in clover,
And life is one beautiful rhyme,

utters a faint thank you when
coins drop near his bony and
bare feet.

I wish you could hear him,
wish you could've found a way
to live without that girl,
who didn't want you.

Death Dancing

I
Outside, it is raining, I chase the drops
with my index finger, following
them as they run down the glass,
crushing the ones I *catch*,

like I wish I could the image of
Mother, small, fragile,
in her king-size bed,
the doctor asking if she has been depressed.
I don't know how to answer.
She married her only love,
retired near her childhood home.

She still sits a place for him at dinner;
I used to remind her that he's gone,
I don't anymore—
I just wash the plate, the white one
with the gray oval spots,
that remind me of deviled eggs.

II
I wish I could crush the memory of the time
I stole gum from Betsy,
took it from her desk during break, was chewing
it when she returned:
I smell watermelon,
the room filling with jays hissing,
Thief! Thief! Thief!

I told her I'd buy more,
she drown while I was at the store,
nothing more was said.

III
When Pamela was found in her room,
wearing a gold sweater, purple parachute pants,
lying among teddy bears
who held umbrellas, balloon bouquets,
wore lilac, antebellum dresses, white hoop slips,
machined laced trim that almost looked handmade,
pillows heading sheets dyed red,
blood flowing from cuts in her neck, her chest.

Our first class was canceled, we were sorted by sex
and age, asked if anyone had tried suicide,
among us: Wrist slitters who couldn't cut deep enough,
Russian roulette players who never chose the right gun,
vodka and sleeping pill shooters who always woke-up.

No one asked who had only thought of suicide,
for those who wore black gowns
to debutant balls, weddings,
danced wild waltzes 'til they were dizzy, backs hurt,
faces ached from silly laughter, to speak.

I wish memories could be buried as easily as bodies.

Portrait of Père Tanguy

On the bus I sat across from a man
in a blue jacket
his large hands rested below his round belly,
beard well trimmed he looks ahead,
like a plastic Santa—

like another man I remember,
from another bus ride I took once.
He was neatly dressed,
though his clothes were worn.

He spent the trip reading, re-reading
a Bible verse printed on a card,
I told my friend about both of them,
she accused me of *idealizing* the men.

She might have been right.
Yet, I can't help thinking both of them
were passing the time lost—
in the wonderment of *what if.*

Tired

> *I was tired of being a woman,*
> *tired of the spoons and the pots,*
> *tired of my mouth and my breasts,*
> *tired of the cosmetics and the silks.*
>   Anne Sexton

I'm tired, not of being female, nor of cosmetics,
I'm tired of artist lining my brows circling my eyes,
debating whether my eye-lids should glitter
in black diamond, or smolder in smoke,
both go well with aubergine,
staining my cheeks the color of burgundy wine,
glazing my lips in a similar hue,
alluding that they taste as sweet,
ending sessions by sprinkling bronze power,
so rich in color I expect it to smell like coco,
I can't mix with my morning milk,

weary of my skin being described as translucent
because my blue veins are visible,
yellow as if I should be ashamed of my ancestors.

On Highway 80

Between Montgomery and Selma
I've seen hay stacked in morning,
at noon, and at night.

Cotton growing so thick
the field looked as if it were covered
with snow.

I've seen the fog lift like a curtain
to reveal a flock of fat buzzards,
with heads tucked beneath wings,
sitting atop a half-circle fence,
like a string of pearls,
around a woman's neck.

Today a thin, matted
coyote crossed the road ahead of me,
and disappeared into an over grown field.

Grand Central Station

I am leaning against a wall
watching people disappear
into the tunnels that return them to trains,
familiar beds.

A tall, thin man with a package in his arms
looks like my cousin Seneca
who spent one day of each month,
waiting for trains to carry him from the suburbs
to bring me a sack of nickels, dimes and pennies,
always saying,
"If you put these in the bank you will have money
for college."

The man in a wheel chair is
reading a crime novel,
like a boy I used to date,
he had Spina Bifida,
he loved to read about serial killers.

A woman wearing a plain white scarf
reminds me of my best friend from high school
who dutifully wore her veil, tunic and pants.
While I sported tight jeans and an occasional
cleavage revealing V cut shirt.

But every morning with outstretched arms,
we greeted each other declaring:
"Darling, you look marvelous!"

Piano Lesson

I read about a man who wanted to trade his savings,
some melons, and a piano built by his enslaved relatives,
for a plot of land.

I imagine the instrument, an upright grand, rich brown
like a Brazil nut's shell, voice warm and inviting
as the host of a gentleman's club
whose members are served from flowing fountains of gin,
and sashaying women whose company come free.

I imagine it sitting on the right hand side
of the 16th Street Baptist Church
during the first Sunday service since the bombing,
a group of women wearing white dresses and yellow roses
comes forward as a voice shouts: *We Shall Over Come!*

The Persistence of Time

The only difference between
me and a madman
is that I'm not mad.
I see time as it is.
Flattened, forced into circular forms
divided into two.
One whose face is always pale, deflated.
Forever, tasked with rearranging
the debris of memory.
Burying the massive body of the platypus
clearing the way so the future
can peel from its casing
and fall as a seed to the earth.

Notes

Evening Guitar:

Bearden, Romare. *Evening Guitar.* 1987. Romare Bearden Foundation.
Tretheway, Natasha. *Domestic Work.* St. Paul: Graywolf Press, 2000.

Railroad Station:

Lawrence, Jacob.

Remembering an Autumn Day:

Hoitsu, Sakai. *Autumn Grasses.* Seattle Art Museum, Washington.
1001 Paintings You Must See Before You Die. Ed. Stephen Farthing. New York: Universe Publishing, 2007. 600.

Apple-Picking:

Pissarro, Camille. *Apple Picking*, 1886. Ohara Museum of Art. Japan. *Impressionism.* Ed. Ingo E. Walther. Los Angeles: Taschen, 2006. pp 275.

Zinnias:

Hunter, Clementine. *Zinnias, Clementine Hunter: American Folk Artist.* James L. Wilson. Louisiana: Pelican, 1990.

Tradition:

Fantin-Latour, Henri. *White and Pink Roses.* 1836. Private Collection. *The Art Book.* New York: Phaidon, 1994. 155.

La Volière:

Ray, Man. *La Volière*.

Dreams 2:

Lawrence, Jacob. *Dreams 2*, Smithsonian American Art Museum.

Madonna and Child:

Clementine. *Madonna and Child, Clementine Hunter: American Folk Artist*. James L. Wilson. Louisiana: Pelican, 1990.
Also, alludes to the 1940 study by Kenneth Bancroft Clark and Mamie Phipps Clark's in which the pair conducted experiments using dolls to study children's attitudes about race.

Dancing Doll:

Bannerman, Helen. *Little Black Sambo*.
Beecher, Stowe Harriet. *Uncle Tom's Cabin*.
Ellison, Ralph. *Invisible Man*. New York: Vintage International, 1995.
Gilman, Rebecca. *Spinning Into Butter*. New York: Giroux, 2000. 430-34.
Lawrence, Jacob. *Dancing Doll*. 1947. Weisman Art Museum. Minneapolis, MN.

Mother's Lessons:

Weir, Walter Robert. *Mothers Lessons, Amalfi, 1857*.

The Floor-Scrapers:

Caillebotte, Gustave. *The Floor-Scrapers*. (*The Floor Strippers*)1875. Musée d'Orsay. Paris. *Impressionism*. ed. Ingo E. Walther. Los Angeles: Taschen, 2006. 131.

Wishing for a Fairy:

Becket-Griffith, Jasmine. *Butterfly Sunset.*

Patience:

Mapplethrope, Robert. *Orchids* ca. 1982.

Ava:

Denmark. James. *Ava*

Montgomery Stairs:

Various historical markers posted around the city of Montgomery as well a couple of lots located in the downtown area, now vacant save for the old residences steps.

Portrait of American Hope:

Malberta Hendricks, Hurricane Katrina survivor. 2005.

Conjure Woman:

Bearden, Romare. *Conjure Woman*. Romare. Bearden Foundation. New York.

Birds of the Bagaduce:

Hartley, Marsden. *Birds of the Bagaduce,* 1939. The Butler Institute of American Art. Youngstown, OH. 1 July 2008.

Seasonal Rain:

Hoitsu, Sakai. *Summer Rain,* National Museum Tokyo. New York: Newsweek. 1968.

South Carolina Morning or Cape Cod Evening:

Hopper, Edward. *South Carolina Morning*, Ed. Ivo Kranzfelder. Los Angeles: Taschen. 2006.
Hopper, Edward. *Cape Cod Evening.* Ed. Ivo Kranzfelder. Los Angeles: Taschen. 2006.

Denial of Appeal:

Vallotton, Felix Edouard. *Three Women and a Young Girl Playing in the Water.* Kunstmuseum, Basel Switzerland.
1001 Paintings You Must See Before You Die. Ed. Stephen Farthing. New York: Universe Publishing, 2007. 570.

Woman in Green Coat:

Macke, August. *Woman in the Green Jacket*.

Still Life:

Harnett, William Henry. *Still Life with Universal Gazetteer.* Museum of Fine *Paintings from the Montgomery Museum of Fine Arts.* Margaret Lynne Ausfeld, Charles C. Eldredge, Mark M. Johnson. Seattle: Marquand Books, Inc. 2006.

Breach of Contract:

Chihuly, Dale. *Blue Venetian with Green Calla Lily. Fire.* Washington: Portland, 2006.

On the Terrace:

Renoir, Auguste-Pierre. *On the Terrace*, 1881. The Art Institute of Chicago. Chicago. *Impressionism.* Ed. Ingo E. Walther. Los Angeles: Taschen, 2006. pp 215.

Self-Examination:

Larsson, Carl. *Self-examination*. Uffizi: Florence. *1001 Paintings You Must See Before YouDie*. Ed. Stephen Farthing. New York: Universe Publishing, 2007. 567.

Cotton Candy:

Children Eating Cotton Candy Miniola Fair, 1946 (Loose-Leaf Photo).

Early Morning:

Balls, Giacomo. *Dynamism of a Dog on a Leash*. Albright-Knox Art Gallery, New York. *1001 Paintings You Must See Before You Die*. ed. Stephen Farthing. New York: Universe Publishing, 2007. pp 600.

Seasonal Longings:

Monet, Claude. *Monet's House at Argenteuil*. *Monet: Impressions of Light*. Ed. Mary Forsell, Joanna Wissinger, Don Kennison. New York: New Line Books. 1996.

Terrace of a Cafe:

Gogh, Vincent van. *Terrace of a Café on Montmartre*. 1886. Musée d'Orsay. Paris. *Impressionism*. ed. Ingo E. Walther. Los Angeles: Taschen, 2006. pp 284-85.

Woman with a Pearl Necklace:

Vermeer, Johannes. *Woman With A Pearl Necklace*. Staatliche Museen, Berlin.

Cornflowers and Ears of Corn:

Faberge, Peter Carl. *Cornflowers and Ears of Corn*. The Hermitage Selected Treasures from a Great Museum. Japan: Dai Nippon, 1990. pp161.

Madame X:

Sargent, John Singer. *Madam X*. Carter Ratcliff. New York: Artabras, 1982. pp 86.

Ballet Dancer:

Degas, Edgar. *Little Dancer of Fourteen Years or Large Dancer, Clothed.*

End of Season:

Chase, William Merritt. *End of Season.* ca. 1885. Mount Holyoke College Art Museum. South Hadley. *Impressionism.* Ed. Ingo E. Walther. Los Angeles: Taschen, 2006. pp 605.

Earth Warming Mexico:

Hartley, Marsden. *Earth Warming Mexico.* Montgomery Museum of Fine Art. Montgomery, AL. *American Paintings from the Montgomery Museum of Fine Arts.* Margaret Lynne Ausfeld, Charles C. Eldredge, Mark M. Johnson. Seattle: Marquand Books, Inc. 2006. pp 165.

Make Your Move:

Holston, Joseph. *Make Your Move.*

Two Note Song:

Jean-Léon Gérôme, Jean-Léon. *A Bath, Woman Bathing Her Feet (Harem Pool)*
Sargent, John Singer. *The Sitwell Family, 1900.* Carter Ratcliff. New York: Artabras, 1982. pp 227.

The Birth of Venus:

Bouguereau, William Adolphe. *The Birth of Venus*, 1879. Musee d'Orsay. Paris. *Impressionism.* Ed. Ingo E. Walther. Los Angeles: Taschen, 2006. pp 188.

After Seeing Agostina Segatori in the Café du Tambourin:

Gogh, Vincent van. *Agostina Segatori in the Cafe du Tambourin.* Rijksmuseum Vincent Van Gogh. Amsterdam. *Impressionism.* Ed. Ingo E. Walther. Los Angeles: Taschen, 2006. pp 287.

Heart Trouble:

Picasso, Pablo. *The Old Guitarist*, 1903. George Evans and Ren Shields. *In the Good Old Summer Time.* 1902.

Death Dancing:

Slevogt, Max. *Dance of Death*, 1896. Germanisches National Museum, Nuremberg. *Impressionism.* Ed. Ingo E. Walther. Los Angeles: Taschen, 2006. pp 447.

Portait of Pére Tanguy:

Gogh, Vincent van. *Portrait of Pere Tanguy.* 1887. Musee Rodin. Paris. Impressionism. Ed. Ingo E. Walther. Los Angeles: Taschen, 2006. pp 293
Gilman, Rebecca. *Spinning Into Butter.* New York: Giroux, 2000.

Tired:

Sexton, Anne. *Consorting with Angels*.

On Highway 80:

Monet, Claude. *Grainstack Haystack Series*

Grand Central Station:

Sloan, John. *Grand Central Station.*1924. Montgomery Museum of Fine Arts., Montgomery, AL. *American Paintings from the Montgomery Museum of Fine Arts*. Margaret Lynne Ausfeld, Charles C. Eldredge, Mark M. Johnson. Seattle: Marquand Books, Inc. 2006. pp 165.
You Look Marvelous. 1985. A song by Billy Crystal

Piano Lesson:

Bearden, Romare. *The Piano Lesson*. 1983. National Gallery of Art. D.C. Wilson, August. *Piano Lesson*. New York: Peguin. 1990.

Persistence of Time:

Dali, Salvadore Dali. *The Persistence of Time.* 1931. The Museum of Modern Art. NewYork. *A Year in Art: A Treasure a Day*. New York: Prestel, 2007.

About the Author

Georgia Ann Banks-Martin was born in Lincoln Park, MI on Feb. 6, 1971. She was raised on the southwest side of Detroit in the area known as Marion Park. She attended Beard Elementary, Wilson Middle School, and Southwestern High. However, she completed high school at Sidney Lanier in 1989 after relocating to Montgomery, AL during the summer of 1988. She earned her BA in English, Language Arts at Huntingdon College, Montgomery, AL (1997) and her M.F.A. (Poetry) at Queens University of Charlotte, located in Charlotte, NC (2009). She and her husband, Roger D. Martin currently live in Montgomery, AL with their dog, Gargoyle and their lovely cats: Nikkie, and Socks.

http://georgiabanksmartin.com
http://artist.to/georgiaannbanks-martin
http://twitter.com/GABanksMartin

Photo by William Frye

www.ingramcontent.com/pod-product-compliance
Lightning Source LLC
Chambersburg PA
CBHW052115070526
44584CB00017B/2491